WORKING IN GOD'S ORCHARD

COLLECTION OF POETRY

BY WILLIE DAVIS

Dorrance Publishing Co
585 Alpha Drive
Suite 103
Pittsburgh, PA 15238
Visit our website at *www.dorrancebookstore.com*

ISBN: 979-8-8852-7250-6
eISBN: 979-8-8852-7695-5

WORKING IN GOD'S ORCHARD

COLLECTION OF POETRY

CONTENTS

BEFORE THE SANDS

As I sit here in my wheelchair,

I look back at all the people who walk back and forth on this warm, sunny day.

My heart is filled with sorrow as I watch the children play;

Oh, how I wish I could run, jump, and play on this warm sunny day.

But my arms are weak, and they always hurt

From pushing on this darn wheelchair.

My hands are so very tiny—

Oh, they're very sore, and they burn and really ache.

As I sit, I began to cry with my head hung very low,

And I think of all the things I used to do before this tragic accident.

Suddenly, a man appears, it seems, from out of nowhere.

He knelt down and wiped away my fears and all my tears.

One tear actually fell and landed smack dab in the middle of his hand.

The tear looked so perfectly round. Oh, how it looked so perfectly clear.

Then the man said the darndest thing that anyone had ever said to me:

"This one lonely tear drop in the palm of my hand

Is worth more to me than a billion grains of sand,

And one day, this teardrop will bring joy across the land.

It will bring love and peace to everyone it meets."

The man arose up off his knees and bid me goodbye,

But I couldn't help but notice the feathers that kept falling from under his coat,

And I wonder for just a split second if this man was a heavenly angel.

I anxiously pushed myself back into the house

To tell my father all that the man had said and done.

My father laughed and gestured for me to get into bed.

He said, "Honey, it was just a kind man who passed you along his way…"

All I could think about was I had met an angel today.

I stood up and put myself into bed,

Then I noticed tears suddenly began to fall from my father's eyes,

But I was so busy and so very tired,

I forgot to give my father his usual kiss and hug.

As I snuggled in the covers and started drifting off to sleep,

I heard my father calling the doctors, and this is what he said,
"It's a miracle, I tell you! It's a miracle today!
Because my child can walk."
So if you see a strange fellow, ever walking down the street,
Please take my advice and check for feathers,
Because you never know who you might meet.

THE ENTERING

I watched the angels as they slowly entered into the church.
They were full of directions
And instructions, too;
And each angel had a special task to do;
And they blessed the holy things, just for me and just for you.
They said God was sending joy
To every woman, man, and child.
He was blessing everything we do.
Aren't you glad God chose you and me?

ANGEL IN THE NIGHT

I was awakened one night during a terrible storm.
I looked around my room, and my soul was frightened.
I saw a shadowy figure standing close by;
It was an angel who just had left God's side.
The angel was weary from the journey it had just partaken.
She said, "God sent me to you, and I hurried, and in fact I even raced.
He said, 'Go tell my child how much I love him and how much I really care
He sent me to comfort you during these troubled times.
He told me to tell you that He heard your prayers,
and He knows what you have bore,
And before you ask, it already has been done.
He is never too busy or too far away
And He never will forsake you, especially in your time of need.
In fact, there's a silver lining awaiting you for all the good things you do;
Stay patient, my child, and please stay strong. Because God loved you way
before you were born.
My job is to stay with you until the storm passes."
And then the angel asked me if I was afraid or lonely.
I answered," Not one little bit.
Now I know that God has answered me, I know I'll be just fine."
Just then, the angel left me and entered into my son's room.
I heard my son say, "Sit down and rest a while. Why don't you kick off your shoes?"
The angel said, "Thank you so much, and what can I do for you?
Do you need anything while I am here?
God wanted me to tell you that He holds you near."
Then I heard my grandson giggling and laughing in his room,
I listened and watched closely while he and the angel played.
When I arose that morning, I asked my family,
"Hey, what did the angel say?"
Everyone looked at me surprised
And astonished by what I had just said.
"Mom, you've been dreaming again.
Or maybe it was something you ate."
Just then, my son said, "Hold up, I had the very same dream too."

Apparently angels do exist;
Or is this a dream that's waiting to come true?
But I'd rather thank God today for His love.
How about you?
Just imagine if God was angry, or even if He was filled with hate.
We all agreed to throw away the tacos from last night,
Just in case!

BABY, SSSH

When baby could not put her shoes on,
She asked her big sister for help.
Then baby said, "Sssh…Ssssh…
Don't tell Grandma. She doesn't know I'm not a big girl yet!"
When baby could not pull her pants down for the toilet,
She asked her big sister for her help.
Then baby said, "Sssh…Sssh…
Don't tell Grandma. She doesn't know I'm not a big girl yet!"
But when baby got tired,
She asked her big sister, "Could you please help?"
Then grandma said, "Sssh…Sssh…
Come here, baby, lay your head on my chest."

BEYOND THE SKIES

The day began to die out
Way before they knew;
The radiance of the sunset gradually came through
With its many colors of hues:
Bright orange, a delicious red, a calming yellow, and velvety blue
That seems to go on forever as it came swiftly bursting through.
As they stood in awe of this beautiful sunset
And all it seemed to do,
They noticed the gray-haired lady as she sat in peace,
As though she saw something beyond the skies.
She would tell us about her father
And how she would tug on her father's pants leg when she was a child
With a big smile on her face.
He would lift her up high in the air, hug her, kiss her, and give her a treat,
And call her his little angel.
When she was angry, she used to stomp her feet and pout her mouth,
And that is when her father would call her his little devil.
He would say, "Devil, you could leave. But not with my child—
She belongs to me."
But when she calmed down, he would tell her about all the good things that
God could do.
She would say His tree could only bear good fruit.
Oh, how she wished her father were here today,
So he could see how his orchard has grown
From that one little seed so long ago.
And his teachings, she would never forget.
She thanked God for blessing her with a wonderful father
That was also His son.
You could tell by the smirk on her face
That it warmed her heart with joy
To pass on her many teachings to all her generations to come.

FOOTPRINTS IN THE SAND
PART 1

One night, I had a dream that I was walking on the beach with God
As I watched scenes of my life flash across the sky,
And as each scene flashed across the sky, I noticed there were two sets of
footprints in the sand:
One set of footprints belong to God, and the other set belong to me.
When the last scene of my life flashed across the sky,
I couldn't help but notice during the lowest and worst times of my life,
There was only one set of footprints in the sand.
This really bothered me
So I turned to God and said, "Lord, why during the worst times of my life
Did you abandon me?
You promised me that you would never leave me or forsake me.
Yet during the most troublesome time of my life
when I needed you the most, there was
Only one set of footprints in the sand."
Then God smiled and turned to me and said, "Oh, my dear precious child
will never leave you. Indeed when you saw only one set of footprints in the
sand those footprints were mine.
That's when I placed you in my arms and carried you."

FOOTPRINTS IN THE SAND
PART 2

While I was standing on the beach with God,

I watched as my life passed me by.

All of life scenes unfolded, right in front of my eyes.

I stood there shaking, and I stood there trembling.

I stood there in total awe.

I was really frightened;

Oh yes, I was really scared.

In fact, I was thinking,

I must be dead.

God knew my every thought, way before I could ask.

God answered me and said, "It is not your time yet."

God said that He was here because He heard my cry.

Then He said, "Try to remember

When you were a child.

Oh how you would search for Me and look towards the sky.

And then you would whisper to Me in such a soft and cute voice.

And then this is what you would say:

'God, is that you, high in the sky?

God, is that you, who just shook that tree?

God, are you here today?

God, are you near?

I know I cannot see your invisible face,

But I also know that you can hear.'"

God said, "You were so sweet then, and you just flourished with grace.

That is why I gave you so many sunny days to play in.

That's why I had to bring you from that dark and horrible place.

I just had to bring you back into the light.

And where I place you is where you need to be.

Because after all, my child, you belong to Me.

I am the beginning, and I am also the end.

And there's no problem too great

Or impossible that I cannot mend."

JUST ASK

The world is full of people running here, running there.
Oh heck! Just people running everywhere!
Oftentimes without too much success,
Only because they just simply did not ask.
The thought never occurred to them,
In God we should put our trust.
Although God never sleeps or slumber,
We sometimes have days that are just plain bummers.
And all we have to do is
Just simply ask, "Oh Lord!
Could you just bring me out of this mess!?"
After all, He truly is the only one who can,
Because when God goes to working, He is really on the case,
And you can rest assured
When He is finished,
The results will be just right,
And the load you thought was heavy
Will suddenly become very light.

A MOTHER'S VIRTUE

To my children:
Please forgive me for all my mistakes.
Through God's grace,
Let me show you what He has done;
Let me show you through God's love.
Children, children,
Oh, my precious seeds:
Let me guide you through my teachings and spoken words;
Let me show you from all my good deeds.
I have made many mistakes
As I watched you grow,
And I learned also from them too.
But after all, my children,
I was a first-time mother,
And you were my newborns,
And now that I am old and all mellow with age,
It feels so nice sitting here, holding my grandson.
I get another chance to mother a child;
Only this time,
It is not filled with so many mistakes.
God must have had a sense of humor
Toward all of mankind;
God must have had a master plan all along,
Because now I am perfect
This time around.

THE ARMORED ANGEL

The angel stood there in God's radiance.
The angel stood there in God's grace.
He stood there with a beautiful smile on his face.
He talked about the wonderful things that God had done.
He stood there boldly with his armor on;
The angel was there to protect us
From all hurt, harm, and danger.
He was there confirming
That God's victory
Is already won.
I stood there in amazement,
All tickled pink;
You could have sworn I was wearing a brand-new mink.
The angel left us good blessings and tidings from above,
But most of all,
The angel left us hope,
And he left us love.

WORKING IN GOD'S ORCHARD
PART 1

One day I went out walking
When God suddenly appeared.
God said He needed someone to help Him,
To help Him grow His trees.
He said good help is so very hard to find these days
And even harder to keep.
Then God said, "You crossed my mind. My dear,
My dear, sweet, precious child.
And this job is not just ordinary work that anyone can do,
But this work requires someone special, someone special just like you."
I was so thrilled and happy that God would even ask,
But I was also thinking, how could I help God,
Help him complete this task?
Then God carried me to His orchard,
Where there stood this magnificent tree.
Oh, it was so grand and beautiful;
It was a pretty sight to see.
I could not help but wonder, wonder to myself,
How could I help God with what appeared to be a very healthy tree?
The tree held a nest in every branch;
Nests of field animals, as well as fowls of the air.
I even saw a cheetah perched high up in the tree, sleeping with a squirrel.
And the tree leaves were so full and hearty and perfectly formed,
And big, succulent fruit hung from the tree branches,
It looked so shiny, and oh—how sweet it smelled!
And the tips of the tree were so high that it actually touched the sky,
And the width was so wide it seemed to stretch for miles.
It was a grand old tree, a grand old tree indeed.

WORKING IN GOD'S ORCHARD
PART 2

All the inhabitants of the Earth were gathered at the tree.
In there, they laid and played in perfect harmony.
The tree attracted everyone to its origins, the old as well as the young.
And everyone loved the smell of the tree; it was the essence of tranquility,
And everyone ate of its fruit.
And the birds sang beautiful melodies; they sang it all day long.
And when nightfall came, that's when the nightingale
Would perch herself high on a branch,
And all the inhabitants of Earth would ask her,
"Now are you ready to sing?"
They always begged her because she sang the sweetest melody.
The nightingale would whisper, "No," because everyone had not come yet
When she sang, you could hear her for miles away.
The melody was so sweet and serene that it put everyone to sleep.
Oh, the sight was so awesome to see that
I could not keep my eyes off that beautiful tree.
Then I turned to God and said, "This tree has everything
This tree seems complete." I asked God, "How did You grow a tree so grand
A tree filled with so much harmony, a tree filled with so much peace?"

WORKING IN GOD'S ORCHARD
PART 3

God said, "Indeed, the tree is grand.
Indeed, the tree is complete.
But this is not the problem; this is not even part of the task."
God turned me around then,
But I kept looking back, looking back at that great, magnificent tree
I had just seen. God pointed to the orchard field
And showed me the trees that really needed help.
All the trees were feeble and broken,
Some dying of disease.
I was so overwhelmed by the sight that I was now seeing.
God and I walked down each row to see exactly what each tree needed.
As we walked, some trees needed water; some were dying of thirst.
Some were planted in soil too tight; some were planted not tight enough.
God and I just kept on walking.
Finally, I said to God what I thought seemed to be the problem:
"This tree is broken and needs mending,
And this tree could use some pruning."
God turned to me and smiled, then He replied, "Exactly, exactly, my child.
That's why I chose you for this special job because you alone would care enough
And give attention to each tree accordingly to its need."
God said, "I must admit, there is plenty of work that must be done.
So I assign special
Angels to you, so that you can complete this task."
Then God was suddenly gone again.
The angels and I began to work right away.
We worked continually around the clock.
We worked in all types of weather; we even worked in the storms,
Covering each tree by night from strong winds and rain.
We even covered them to protect them from the cold.
We worked on our hands and knees until they were all bloody and worn.
At the end of the orchard, there were trees caught up in brier
Wrapped all around them, choking the very life from them,
But not one angel or I ever complained, and no one even moaned,
Because we were so happy to do the work that God had placed upon us.

WORKING IN GOD'S ORCHARD
PART 4

On very hot days, we would sit under God's great tree.
Because it was so shady and cool, it felt just like someone had
an air conditioner on.
And oh, when storms came and really were at their worst,
We would run to God's magnificent tree
because the ground around it was always dry,
And it really kept us warm.
Then we would go back to work after the worst of the storm had passed,
So that we could finish our task.
Finally the day had come when God came to see us.
He came to see just how much work we had done.
God stood there with a great, big smile on His face.
He said, "My children, my children, indeed this is a job well done."
Then God turned and said unto me,
"Oh, I have been watching you for quite a while.
I've even been watching you from a far.
I remember the very first time that I brought you to my orchard.
I even remember the very first tree you cared for.
It was the smallest and the very weakest tree of them all.
I watched you as you dropped
Down to your knees with tears rolling down your eyes.
I watched you tend to that tree so carefully as joy swelled up in my heart."
God said, "Now look at your tree. See how it has waxed so mighty and strong.
I have been seeing new creatures move into that tree,
Building their nests. You can tell they are happy to have found a new home.
I saw a little girl jumping rope under your tree. The angels and I love
To see her play because every time the wind would blow
She would become perfectly still, and I could hear her whispering softly to me
I even saw a little gray-haired lady, sitting there in peace."
God said, "When I first brought you to the orchard,
you asked me about my great tree.
You were curious about how the tree grew so strong.

Now I am going to give you the answer to the question you have asked.
Now that your job is all done,
I planted that great tree with just one little seed.
But that is not what made the tree grow.
The only thing that all the trees really needed all along
Was just someone to care for them and nurture them with love.”

END OF THE SANDS

While I was standing on the beach with God,
I watched the very last scenes of my life passing through the sky.
It was a scene of grandchildren who had not yet come
But were coming soon.
I watched patiently as my generation grew,
And a scene of a little, gray-haired lady who had a twinkle in her eye, or
maybe even two.
It was a vision of myself sitting under the tree, reading the Bible to all my seeds.
Then I realized exactly what was the purpose of the great tree.
It was a tree I dreamed about a long time ago
When I walked with God through His orchard.
The water kept changing its hues
As it glistened like sparkling jewels.
I was wishing somehow that none of the things I saw would ever come to an end
The day came to an end with me walking alone on the beach
As I headed straight for home,
And all I could think about in my mind was, *That was a heck of a dream!*
As I laid in my bed, awakened by the sound of a telephone ring.

PARADISE

Pink, lavender, and yellow skies;
Laughing and dancing dolphins
Jumping in and out of tides.
Tropical fishes swimming and playing;
Crushed diamonds and pearls scattered along the seashore.
Sparkling, and dazzling rainbows streaked across the sky;
Golden sunsets with cool summer breezes that gently caress.
And with a twinkling of the eye,
It suddenly disappeared
With an alarm clock ringing loudly in my ears.
Babies crying, screaming, and demanding something sweet to eat.
A sink full of dishes that I had not washed yet.
That's when I looked around at the paradise that I was in.
Oh, how I wished I could go back to sleep,
Just so I could dream that beautiful dream all over again.